THE NATURE KIDS GUIDE TO

PRONGHORNS

DAVID ANDERSON

LP Media Inc. Publishing
Text copyright © 2026 by LP Media Inc.
All rights reserved.

For information address LP Media Inc. Publishing,
30012 Variolite St NW, Princeton MN 55371
www.lpmedia.org

Publication Data

Pronghorns
The Nature Kid's Guide to Pronghorns — First edition.

Summary: "Learn all about Pronghorns, the Nature Kid Way"
— Provided by publisher.

ISBN: 979-8-89818-152-9

[1. Pronghorns – Non-Fiction] I. Title.

Title: The Nature Kid's Guide to Pronghorns

CONTENTS

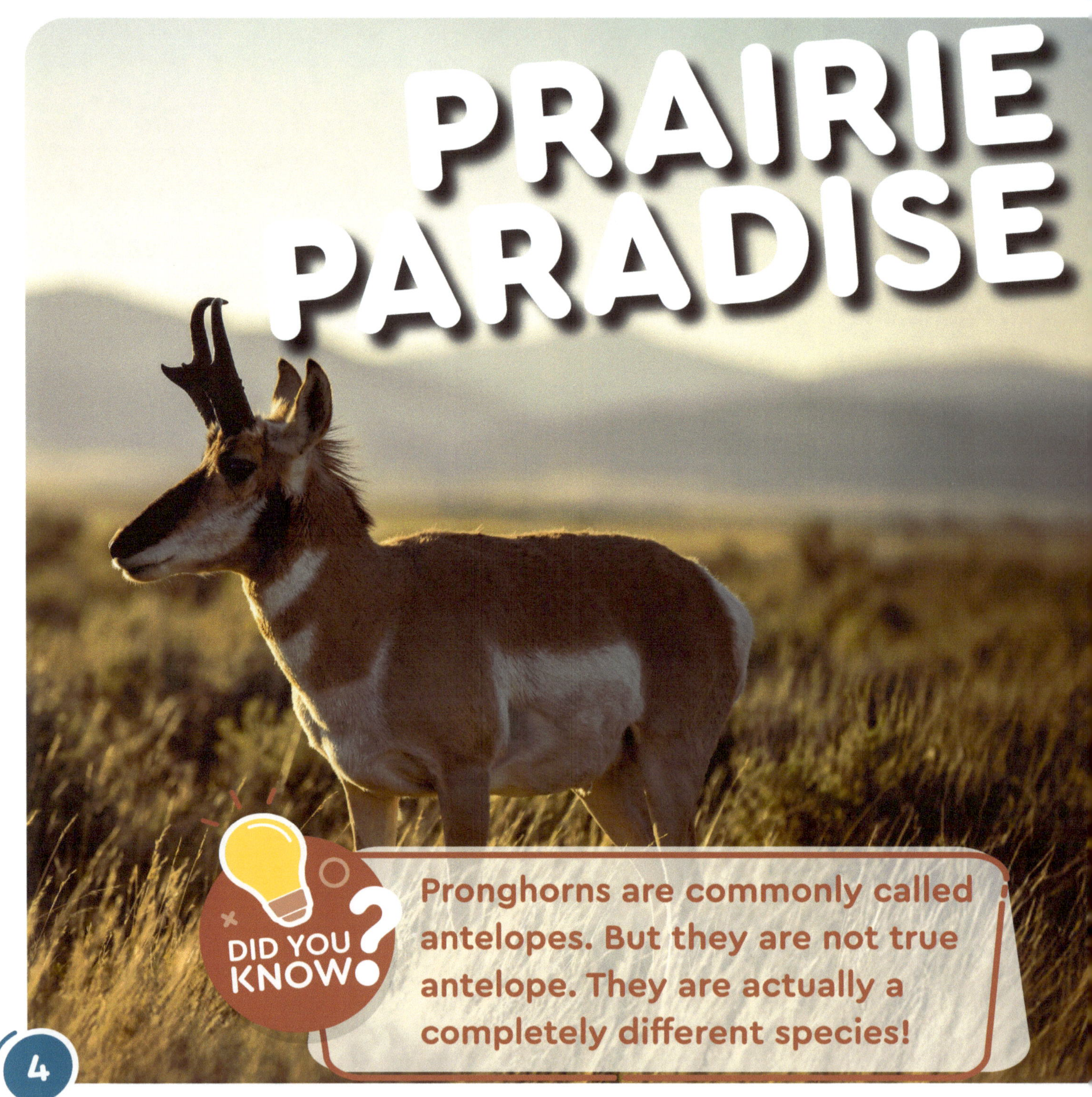

PRAIRIE PARADISE
DID YOU KNOW?
Pronghorns are commonly called antelopes. But they are not true antelope. They are actually a completely different species!
4

Whoosh! Wind sweeps across the plains. A pronghorn lifts its head to watch.

Pronghorns make their homes on **prairies** and grasslands. These wide, flat areas have few trees. Pronghorns use open spaces to spot danger up to 4 miles away.

The habitat stays dry for most of the year. Short grasses and shrubs cover the ground. Sagebrush grows in many areas where pronghorns live. This plant gives them food and shelter.

Pronghorns also live in high deserts. Some live on flat land over 8,000 feet high. Their habitat can reach 100°F in summer! They survive both hot summers and cold winters.

PRAIRIE LIFE

Thump! Hooves hit the dusty trail. A pronghorn trots on.

Pronghorns live in western North America. They roam from southern Canada to northern Mexico.

Most pronghorns stay in the United States. Wyoming has the most pronghorns. Montana and Nevada have many herds too.

Some pronghorns **migrate** each year. They travel up to 150 miles. They move between summer and winter homes.

Pronghorns once roamed all of western North America. Millions lived on the plains.

SIZE CHECK

Snap! A twig breaks. A pronghorn stands alert in the grass.

Pronghorns stand about 3 feet tall at the shoulder. They are smaller than deer.

Female pronghorns weigh 75 to 105 pounds. Males can weigh up to 140 pounds.

Pronghorns have slim bodies and long legs. Their bones are hollow, making them even lighter. This light build helps them run fast. Everything about their body is made for speed.

Pronghorns have long black eyelashes. They work like sunglasses to protect their eyes from the bright sun.

BUILT TO BOLT

Click! Hooves tap on rocky ground. A pronghorn stretches its long neck.

Pronghorns have special bodies for running. Their windpipe is extra wide. This lets them breathe in lots of air while they sprint.

Their hearts are very large for their size. A big heart pumps more blood to muscles. Big lungs help too, giving muscles the air they need.

Pronghorn legs have long bones and strong **tendons**. Their hooves are cushioned inside, which helps them run on hard ground without getting hurt. Every body part helps them move fast.

SUPER SIGHT

Swoosh! A pronghorn scans the wide prairie. Its huge eyes never blink.

Pronghorns have amazing eyesight. Their eyes are as big as an elephant's eyes! Eyes this large help them spot danger from far away.

Each eye sits on the side of the head. This lets pronghorns see almost all around them.

They can spot movement up to 4 miles away. This gives them plenty of time to run before a predator gets close.

Pronghorn eyes have special cells that can detect tiny movements.

FLASH
WARNING

Puff! White fur flashes bright. A pronghorn raises its rump patch.

Pronghorns have a special warning system. White hairs on their rump can stand straight up. This makes a bright flash that other pronghorns can see.

The white patch becomes larger and puffy when raised. Pronghorns up to 2.5 miles away can notice this signal.

The flash works like an alarm. When one pronghorn flashes, others flash too. The warning spreads quickly across the herd.

The white rump hairs puff up in just 3 seconds! Tiny muscles lift each hair.

15

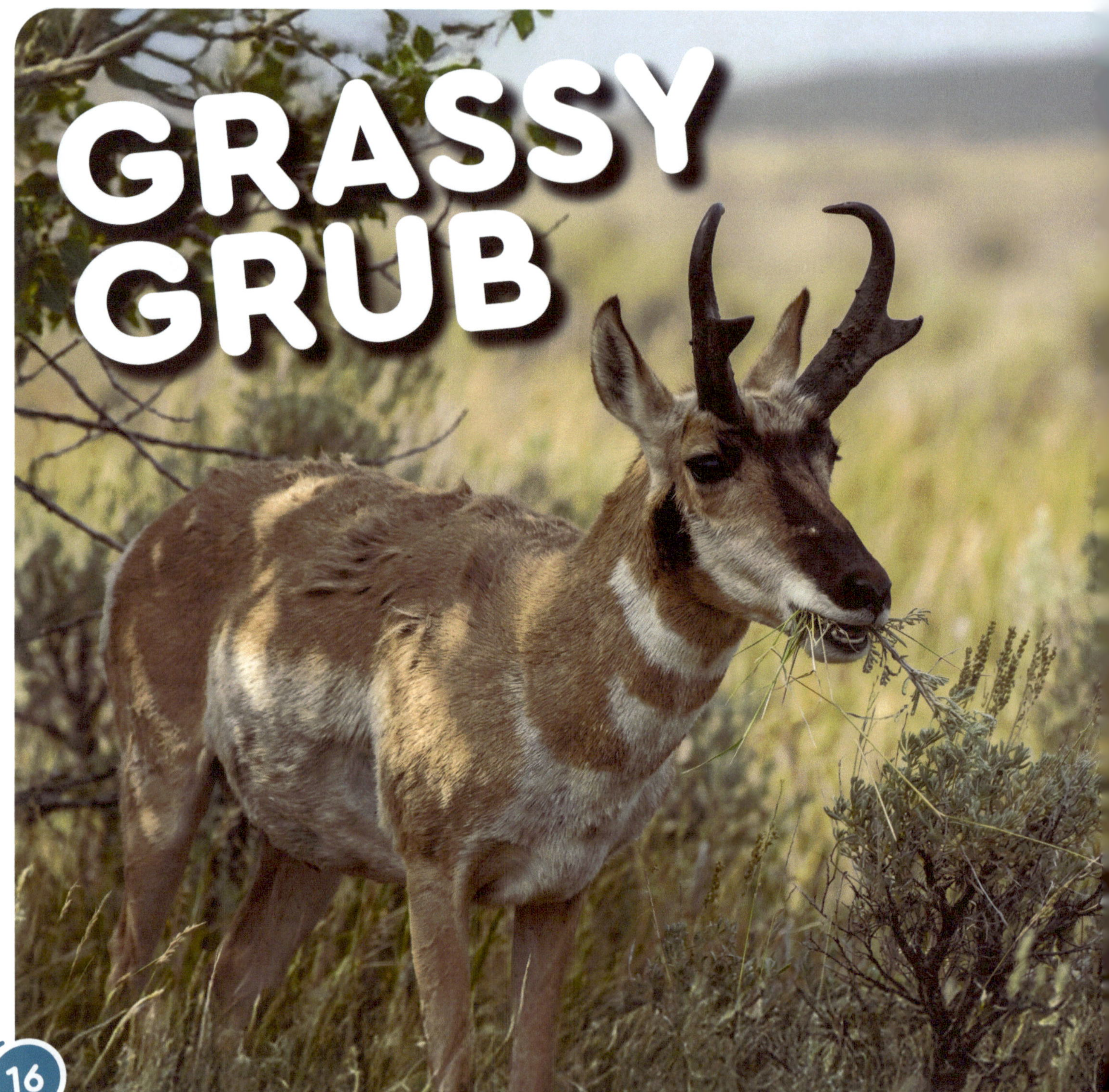

GRASSY GRUB

Crunch! A pronghorn bites off a mouthful of plants.

Pronghorns eat many kinds of plants. They munch on grasses, weeds, and shrubs. Sagebrush is one of their favorite foods.

These animals are not picky eaters. They nibble on whatever plants grow nearby. In summer, they eat more flowers and soft plants.

In winter, food is harder to find. Pronghorns dig through snow to reach plants. They can eat plants that other animals won't eat.

Pronghorns get most of their water from plants. They can go for weeks without taking a drink!

SNORTS AND SIGNALS

Males have scent glands on their cheeks. They rub these on plants to mark territory.

Snort! A pronghorn calls out. Others turn to listen.

Pronghorns talk to each other in many ways. They make snorting sounds to warn of danger. A loud snort tells the herd to pay attention.

They also use smells to send messages. Pronghorns have special **scent glands** on their rumps. These glands release smells that other pronghorns can detect.

Body movements share information too. A pronghorn may stomp its foot when nervous. It might also bob its head up and down. These signals help the herd stay safe together.

PROWLING PREDATORS

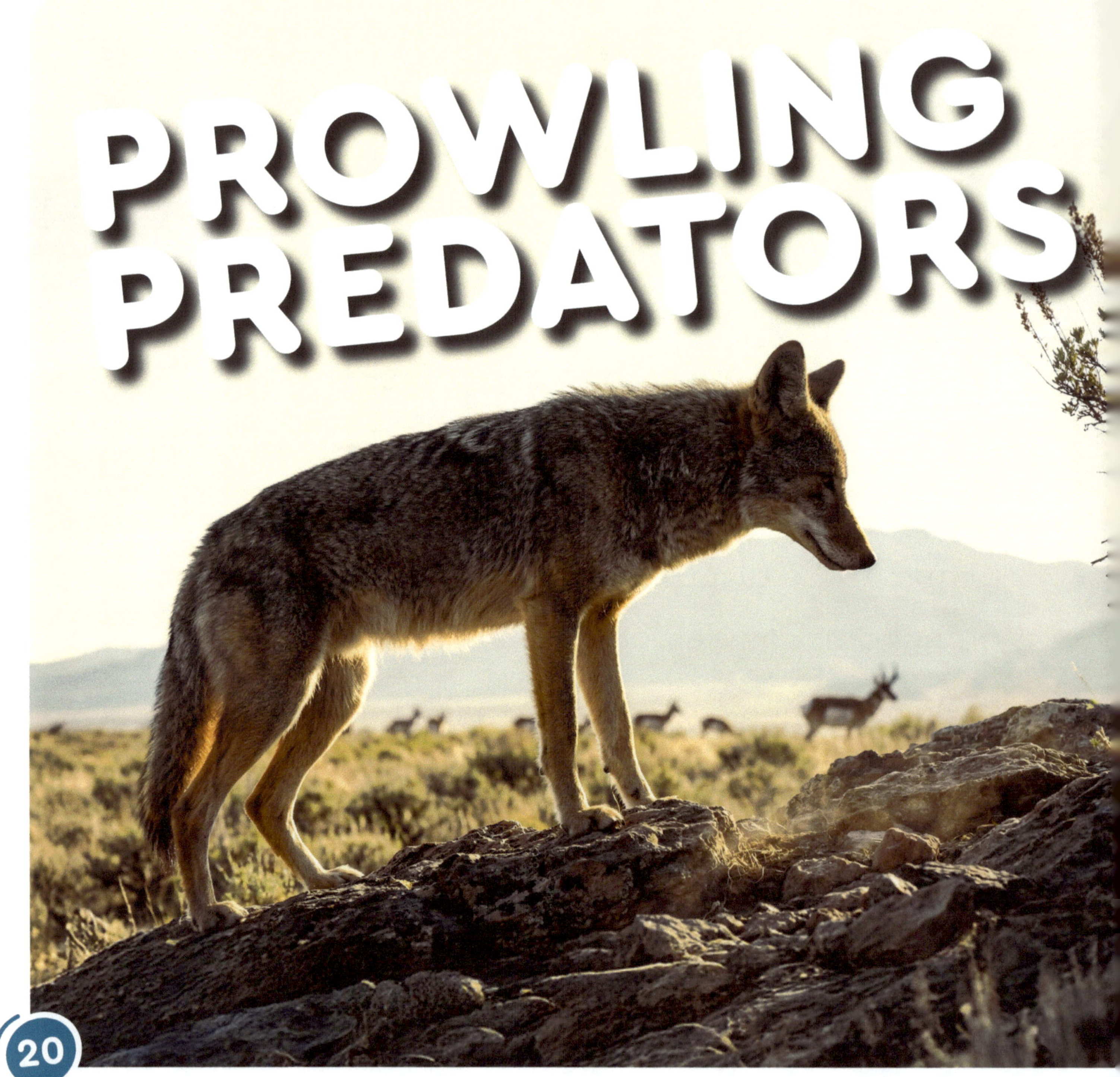

Howl! A coyote watches from a hill. It eyes the herd below.

Pronghorns face danger from several predators. Coyotes hunt pronghorns on the open prairie. Golden eagles swoop down from the sky.

Wolves also chase pronghorns in some areas. Mountain lions hide and wait to pounce on passing prey.

Young fawns face the most danger. Bobcats and coyotes hunt them often. But adult pronghorns use their speed to escape most predators.

Golden eagles can dive at speeds over 150 miles per hour to catch their prey.

ZOOM AWAY

Zoom! A pronghorn runs fast across the flat land.

Pronghorns are good at getting away. They can run 35 miles per hour. They can keep this up for 4 miles!

These animals do not hide. They do not fight. They just outrun enemies. A pronghorn can run for miles and miles.

Herds run together when scared. Young pronghorns follow the adults. Running as a group keeps them all safe.

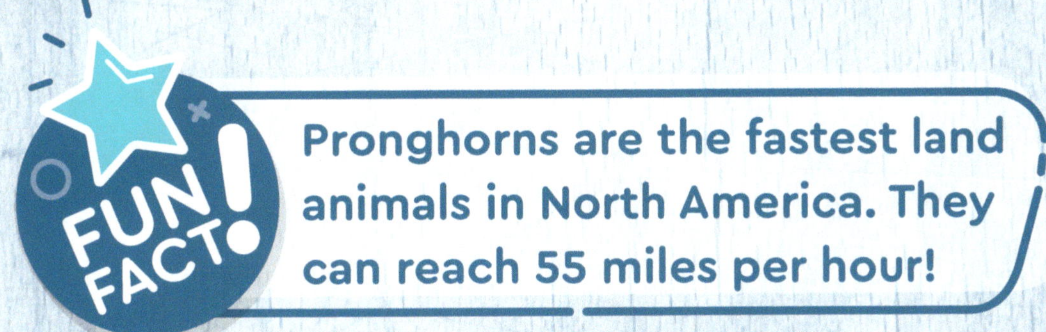

Pronghorns are the fastest land animals in North America. They can reach 55 miles per hour!

SPEED
STARS

Rumble! Hooves thunder past. A pronghorn races by.

Pronghorns are the fastest land animals in North America. They can run up to 55 miles per hour.

Their bodies are made for running. Large lungs take in lots of air. A big heart pumps blood quickly to their muscles.

Pronghorns can keep up fast speeds longer than almost any other animal. They can run at top speed for half a mile before they need to slow down.

Pronghorns can run fast when they are just days old. Week-old babies can outrun a human!

DAY BY DAY

Rustle! Grass bends in the breeze. A pronghorn begins its day.

Pronghorns are most active in the early morning and late afternoon. They spend these cooler hours eating and moving around.

During the hot midday sun, pronghorns rest. They lie down in groups and chew their cud.

Pronghorns sleep in short bursts of less than 10 minutes. They wake often to check for danger. Sometimes they even sleep with their eyes open!

Pronghorns chew their cud about 40 times before swallowing. This helps break down tough plants.

HERD
HANGOUT

Grunt! A pronghorn joins the group. Now many eyes watch together.

Pronghorns live in herds. A herd can have 5 to 1,000 animals. Living together helps them spot danger faster.

In summer, females and young form their own groups. Males often stay in small bachelor herds.

In winter, many herds join together. These large groups travel to find food in the snow.

Herds often follow an older female. Any member can start moving, and others follow.

SHOWING OFF

Stomp! A male pronghorn struts across the prairie.

Male pronghorns compete for females each fall. They puff up their cheeks and make loud snorting sounds.

Males also mark their territory with scent. Remember those scent glands on their rumps and near their eyes? This smell tells other males to stay away.

When warnings don't work, males chase and push each other. The strongest male gets to stay with the females.

Females often stay with a male for only a few days before moving to another male.

FAWN FRIENDS

Pronghorn babies are called fawns. They are born in late spring when food is plentiful.

Newborn fawns weigh about 7 pounds. Their grayish-brown fur helps them hide in grass and brush. They also stay very still to avoid predators.

Fawns can stand within 30 minutes of being born. After just a few days, they can outrun a human!

They grow quickly. A fawn can double its weight in just a few weeks. This fast growth comes from their mother's rich milk.

GROWING UP

A young pronghorn trots beside its mother on the open prairie.

Fawns grow fast on the prairie. They nurse for about three months. Then they start eating plants like the adults.

Young pronghorns stay close to their mothers for about a year. During this time, they learn where to find food and water.

Females usually stay with their mother's herd. Males leave when they are about one year old. They join bachelor groups until they are fully grown.

DID YOU KNOW?

Twin fawns are common! About 60% of births are twins.

BORN SURVIVORS

Crack! Ice breaks on a pond. A pronghorn takes a drink.

Pronghorns are tough. They live through very cold winters and very hot summers. They grow a thicker coat for winter, then shed it in spring.

Their bodies stay warm or cool in smart ways. Their hairs are hollow. The hairs trap warmth in winter. Their fur is light in color. It reflects sun in summer. Pronghorns can also raise their hair to let heat escape, like opening a window!

Pronghorns live in temps that range from -50 to over 100 degrees Fahrenheit!

SPOT ONE

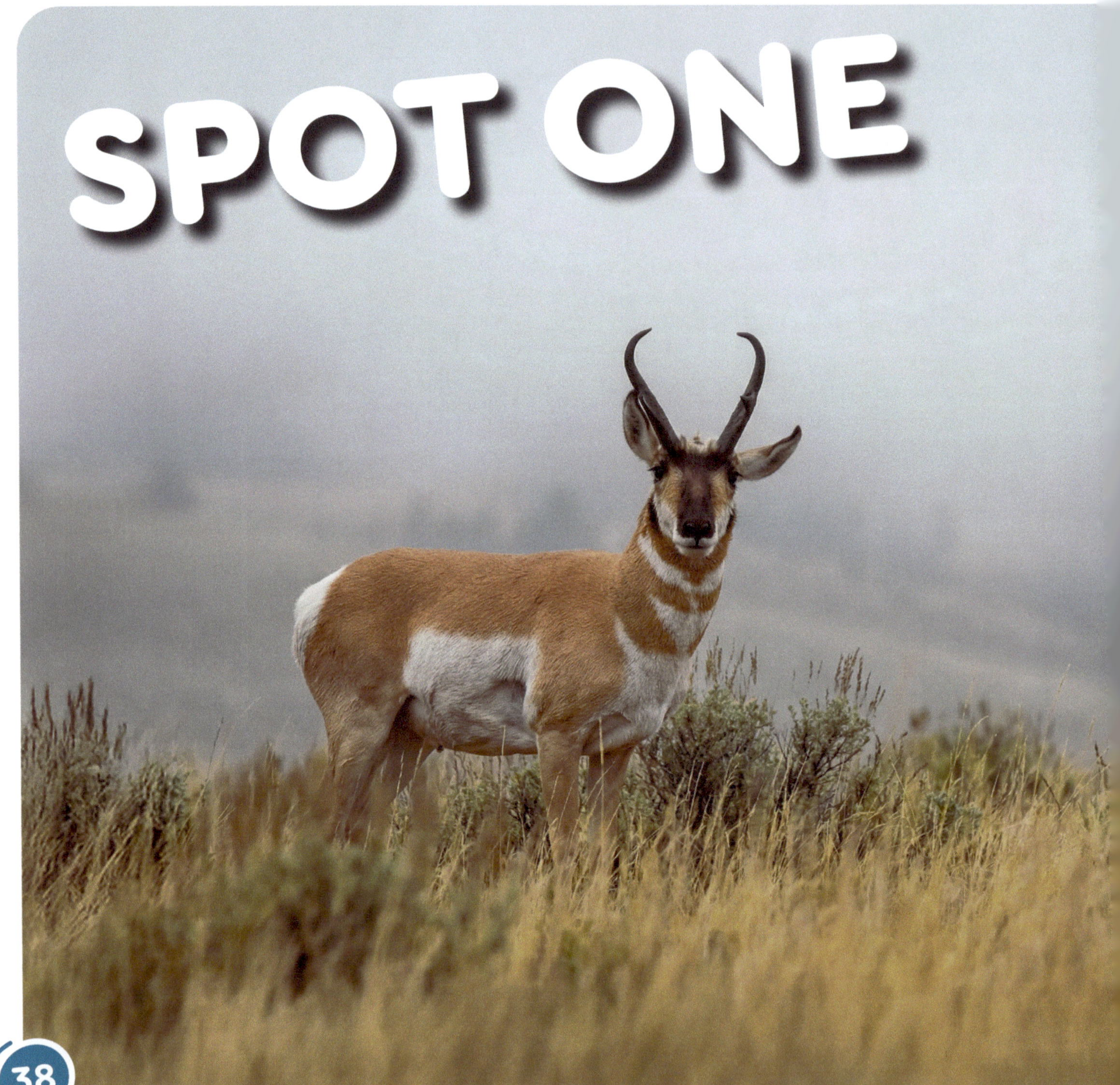

Tall grass parts. A pronghorn stands still, it's watching you.

Want to see a pronghorn? Visit grasslands in their home range in the early morning or late afternoon. That is when they are most active.

You will need binoculars! Pronghorns can spot movement from up to 4 miles away. If they see you close they will bolt away! Stay in your car or hide behind bushes.

Look for their white rump patches. These bright spots stand out against the brown grass.

National parks like Yellowstone are great places to watch pronghorns in the wild.

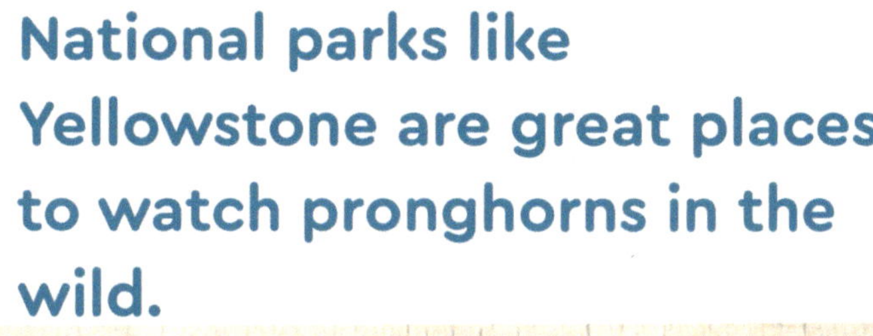

GLOSSARY

prairie
A big, flat area of land covered mostly with grass and very few trees.

migrate
To travel a long way from one home to another when seasons change.

tendons
Strong, stretchy parts inside your body that connect muscles to bones.

scent glands
Special body parts that make smells animals use to send messages.

predators
Animals that hunt and eat other animals for food.